STIJN HEYMANS

CHANGE YOUR LIFE IN SIX STEPS

Copyright

Author book: Stijn Heymans
Title: Change your life in six steps

Cover: Eva Daeleman

© Year 2019, Author Stijn Heymans
Self-published
www.stijnheymans.be

Contact: stijn@stijnheymans.be

Index

Change your life in six steps

From mediocre to awesome

Are you having trouble finding your way to live the best version of your life?

Well, I have designed a roadmap for you!

I went through my journey and discovered how I could live my version of life. Instead of you going through some rough life lessons too, I have created this book for you so you can anticipate and start creating some awesomeness right now!

Get ready to change your life – because it will happen.

> *We only learn through mistakes, but they do not have to be ours. We only learn through hard work, but it does not have to all be our hard work.*
> *- Warren Buffet*

Curriculum

Introduction
Act upon the feeling that you need a change in your life!
Find out how the process of change works and take it into
practice in your life. Move towards your awesomeness!

Chapter 1 – Where you are
Get a clear vision upon your current life that asks for
change.

Chapter 2 – Know what you want
You will have a clear overview of where to direct your
energy.

Chapter 3 – Unconscious to conscious
You will be aware that everything that happens is created
by yourself, conscious, or unconscious. Knowing that you
will be able to learn why things are happening so you can
act upon them.

Chapter 4 – Everything is possible
You will learn to dream big, without limitations. Everything
is possible. You will have a better point of view on what you
desire when you dare to dream big.

Chapter 5 – Choose your life

You will develop your way of believing and manifesting your dreams/awesomeness. A daily routine that suits your lifestyle and personality. You will have a practical guide that empowers yourself, gives hope and inspires.

Chapter 6 – Everything is a choice

You will learn how you can implement a new habit into your life and keep it alive.

Chapter 7 – Law of attraction

You will learn that sharing is caring and that you can contribute to a collective while taking care of yourself at the same time.

Live your awesome life

You will have all the tools, tips, and trick to transform anything you want into awesomeness. Create your version of "an awesome life."

Introduction

Awesome! Let's go!

Are you ready to start traveling your inner world and change your outer world? Your reality? Because that is literally what you are going to do when starting this journey together with me.

I am sharing with you a starter's guide that is accessible for everyone, pro's and beginners, and whoever feels that they need change within their lives.

Learning outcome

Act upon the feeling that you need a change in your life! Find out how the process of change works and take it into practice in your life. Move towards your awesomeness!

Who am I

First things first: who am I, and why did I create this course? Let me explain!

My name is Stijn Heymans, and my business card states: "philanthropist." Stijn is a Belgian/Dutch name and here is the trick to pronouncing it correctly: just like, you would pronounce "Stan" in English. S T A N.

After 26 years of living my life as a positive person, I discovered that there is much more than living a life in automatic pilot mode. I found that I could choose what I want to do. No limitations, fearless, and ego. However, living MY 100% awesome life is what I am aiming for right now. It was already some years ago that I got this insight or lesson, which taught me that I could create my own life.

So allow me to explain how I lived a former "automatic pilot-mode" life.

When I was 19, a precious person – someone with whom I had a sincere connection - killed herself. I was devastated. To some people, big (bad) things happen in their lives, and after that, they completely change the way they live. I thought that I did the same, but actually, I made it even worse and was not able – yet - to learn my lesson from that experience.

Before, life was my playground, and nothing could stop me. Experimenting as a teenager, figuring out what I wanted to achieve or what I had to offer to the world. All standard stuff but with one crucial notion: I was exploring and figuring out **my** way in life. Following my intuition, since our educational system is not teaching us how to figure out what you want in life or how you can discover your passion. I

After that suicide, something changed in my lifestyle. I became paralyzed and was so confused that I started to live more and more in an automatic pilot mode. Whereas I questioned "life as we know it" as a teenager and tried to follow my guts since then, I cut myself off my intuition. I based myself upon a blueprint-of-success that society had created for me: become good at what you do, get a degree, find a girlfriend, go into business life, work five days a week, 8 hours a day, sometimes go on a holiday, buy a house, … you get the point.

I have gone through many life lessons to realize finally that it is possible to choose my direction in life. I made choices, made mistakes, had some wins, and had some losses. After my 'automatic pilot adolescence life,' to the outer world, all looked ideal in my every day outer life. I had a well-paid job, a girlfriend, a renovated house, an occasional vacation, but in my inner world, all went down. Eventually, my body suffered from it all: I had many back pains, and I did not get any sleep. I had stress from not living my life to the fullest.

What happened to me at that time was a big wake-up call that I could not ignore. Everything changed: work, relationships, housing... my complete lifestyle. I went all-in into figuring out what I wanted in life and did lots of self-development in discovering the unseen world for me. It was, and still is, a bumpy road. On paper everything seems so easy. But in real life it's always harder. I definitely had to bring in my A-game and kept pushing my comfort zone.

I could go into detail what happened and what my life lessons were, but that would not serve you at all.

It is not about the thing that happened; it is the impact that it leaves upon your life. In my case: I lost a precious life-partner, someone else may have lost a dog. Who am I to judge what has the most impact!

As I will discuss later in the book, you have to create your **own** life, and each individual gets to learn a specific something out of experiences. However, it all comes down to this: live your own most awesome life!

I feel privileged that I already got the insight that I can create anything I want at my age now (born in 1988 that is). Some people realize it younger, and some realize it when they are older. When they are 25, 35, 40, 50, 60, Years old and that is fine too! By re-evaluating everything in my own life and learning how to be 100% myself, I discovered a passion within myself to share these insights with many people to let them know how awesome it feels to be 100% themselves.

My vision is that no one needs to look for their awesome selves after x-years of life experience. I want that while we are growing older, we already know who we are and what we use our supernatural powers all the time! Just be the most awesome version of yourself all the time, from day 1 of your existence.

ARE YOU READY?

No? You are not ready. That is also fine too. I have designed this book in such a way that you can pick it up whenever it feels right for you. Therefore, if you want, you can just come back some other time when it does feel right. This book will always be waiting here, waiting for you to start the process of change. However, if the first feeling is a "No" when I ask you, are you ready, keep on reading until the end of this chapter. It could be that your No means. Yes, I am SO ready!

There is a chance that you are feeling some resistance or doubt when I ask you the question, "Are you ready?" That is a good sign. You **feel** that you want to change, but - as you might know - the human body does not always *like* changes. Even not if it is changing towards something "more awesome."

It is brave to go for a change and to take responsibility for your life by starting to create what you want for yourself! I'm still scared when I'm pushing my boundaries. By publishing this book for example. Do I want this: yes. Am I fearless and is all going as smooth as possible: not at all.

Therefore, if your "no" was based upon resistance/fear or doubt about change, then you are ready to go!

Having said all of the above, you probably start to notice that one of the essential aspects in changing something in your life/reality really wants it. We will talk more about "what you want" in one of the next chapters.

For now, you have found this book, and you are reading this, it probably means that you are ready for change. You want it that much, and now you are surrounding yourself with teachings/books/lectures/... Heaven yeah! Let us start creating something extraordinary!

Pre-requisites, not needed

This book is a guide that can be applied by anyone, and no pre-requisites are required. You can be a well-trained yoga practitioner, have plenty of meditation experience, or have no experience at all. All is good, and I will walk you through it. The depth of impact that this experience will have on you is in your hands. However, always realize that you are in control and you get to decide!

The cool thing about these "six steps to change your life" is that it suits everyone and every situation. You can use this guide over and repeatedly again to deepen the practice and to manifest new things. That means that over time – when the practice becomes your lifestyle – you will be able to manifest amazing things in a short amount of time (yes, big life-changing manifestations too!).

How I designed the program

I have designed a visual template "Change your life in 6 steps," which represents the simple steps to make the change to something better.

How to make
everything awesome
In 6 simple steps

Where you are   START
This is the starting point.
What are you doing right
now that you are going to
change?

STEP
01   Know what you want
Listen to your inner self and all
the signals of life. What do you
want at this moment in your life?

Unconscious to
STEP
02
conscious
Become aware of everything
you do. What are you creating
now from your unconscious?

STEP
03   Everything is possible
Dare to dream big and realize
everything IS possible. What
kind of believe is limiting your
creation?

Choose your life!
STEP
04
Start creating your
awesomeness. What actions
are you taking?

STEP
05   Everything is a choice
Things aren't happening to you, you
are choosing to experience them. Is
there something that feels like you
are having no choice?

Law of attraction
STEP
06
Surround yourself with what you
want to become so your reality
can shift towards it. Write down
the things you will surround
yourself with.

FINISH   Live your
awesome life
Enjoy it to the fullest!
Return to start if you want to manifest
something new!

You can get a digital copy of it on my website www.
stijnheymans.be/sixsteps. It is a good thing to print that
sheet out for yourself and put it somewhere where it gets
your attention every day. On the mirror, on the table where
you have breakfast, I will explain every step more into detail
during our time together. I will walk you through each step
individually — six steps to transfer your current situation
into awesomeness. Including the start and endpoint, leaves
us with eight steps in total.

The printed version will be a good reference through the
whole practice. It will remind you every day what you are up
to and which direction you are directing your energy.

Timing

Eight days – 1 week – 1 month – 1 day - ... There is no
right or wrong when it comes to timing. Theoretically, it
is possible to go through all of the steps within minutes.
However, out of the experience, it might take some more
time. However, the time it will take is up to you and the
kind of greatness you want to manifest. Changing your
life is a process. Enjoy that process, so time is somehow
irrelevant. Just make sure you get to the final step in a time
that feels good for yourself. Keep on applying the powerful
tools, tips, and tricks repeatedly and over again!

My suggestion on timing is to have a look at one chapter
a day. Which means that after a week, you will have
everything you need to create something new.

If you feel that, you need to spend more time on a specific chapter: totally fine, take your time and move on when you feel ready.

One week of training that teaches you how to change everything into awesomeness. Isn't THAT awesome!

I strongly advise you to integrate the teachings into your everyday life and do not see this as an individual course.

I will be sharing with you a lifestyle. A lifestyle where you won't settle for less than 100% because you realize that you can choose whichever life you want to live. I cannot see how you would not want to live such a lifestyle and make it just a temporary practice. I want to highlight this really clear, and it is a lifestyle. Not just a short retreat or a one-time study. After going through it all, you keep on doing it. Why? Because you **want** it. You want to get the best out of your life.

The goal is to spend about 20-30 minutes a day in one chapter. I do recommend making it a daily practice of 20 minutes instead of once a week practice of 140 minutes. Create a routine for yourself. You want something to change, so you want to put energy towards that change **every single day**. It is worth it.

As always, you have to stay connected with your being. If you feel you need a break, allow yourself to have that break. More of creating a new habit will be discussed in one of the upcoming chapters: Everything is a choice - How to implement a new habit

Are you all in? "All in" means that you are willing to pay attention to every aspect of life during the time that you are manifesting. By doing this, you will be able to feel/see more results in a shorter period. One of the aspects that I highly recommend you to pay attention to is food. Are you willing to be all in and feed your body with only the best, so you have plenty of energy to focus upon manifesting what you want?

Life force

Look at it this way: there is an unlimited amount of energy available for everyone. Let us give it a name: life force.

When there is something in your life that you want to change, you are currently using that life force on something that you do not want. Right?

The goal is to direct that same life force towards something (new) awesome that you want to manifest. In addition, for that transformation, you need lots of energy since you are going to stretch your comfort zone. You are going to discover your own rules/visions in life. How you want to see it, instead of assuming that everything you have learned is correct (such as you **must** work hard to earn money). Changing your beliefs and accessing your full potential takes more energy than just sitting in the couch of your comfort zone. That is why it can be really (really?) empowering to pay attention to food because you need more energy during these times!

I highly recommend you to be all in.

I will talk about food and how to pay attention to it later on!

My intention

I intend to inspire you and to dare you to dream big. That is why I am continuously pushing the boundaries of your beliefs and patterns. When I'm giving you a "theoretical" explanation such as "It IS possible to take all of the six steps within minutes or seconds and manifest crazy, unbelievable things in a snap" I am doing this intentionally to prove a point to you. When I discovered the power of manifestation, I never imagined myself living the life I am living now, and the speed that literally changed everything. Even now, after practicing these six steps for years and while sharing it with you now, I feel and believe that there is much more possible than what I am manifesting for myself now.

This is why I want to be very clear when I share with you this course. I want to share what I have discovered, and that is, everything is possible, even the impossible. The impossible only looks impossible, but it will become possible soon if you start working on your limiting beliefs. It is your own belief that is holding you back from manifesting the so-called "impossible."

Enjoy the process

Very important! Transform into awesomeness with a smile. This guide is a practice that shows you how you can transform everything. Does this mean that after going through it all it will be transformed in seven days...? Maybe... If not, keep on applying the teachings from each step repeatedly. Gain trust and faith in the transformational process.

Since it can be that it will take more than some days, enjoy the process. You are not being forced to change something in your life. You **want** it, remember?

Doing it with a smile improves the whole experience, so why would you do it otherwise?

Enjoy the ride...!

At first, we are going to map the current situation where you are right now in your life. It is a good practice to put down in words what it is you want to change. Be specific! Later on, it will be a good starting point to see and feel what you want!

Let us get started!

First, you will go more into detail of the current situation, and by the end of this book, you will have a more clear view of what you want to change! You must listen very clearly to yourself/your own being/your own body, that is the first thing to do in almost every situation: listen.

As you have started to read, this book is already a proof that you can listen to yourself. You **feel** that something needs to change, and you take action on that. However, keep in mind that the first thing that you have done was, listening.

The cool thing about you reading this book is that you used your intuition intuitively. You listened to it. Now here is the one million dollar question: can you listen to your intuition whenever you want to?

Or more importantly, can you ask your intuition questions when you need answers?

My answer to that is clear: Heaven yeah, that is possible. Moreover, that is what I want you to do in this first chapter. Ask yourself what it is that you want to change. What is it that is bothering you at this very moment?

> *Start the positive.*
> *Do not fix the negative.*

Learning outcome

Get a clear vision upon your current life that asks for change.

Where are you now?

It all may sound hard and strange to "listen to your intuition," but in fact, it is easy.

For this first chapter, I will guide you through how to put it all on a piece of paper. Which you can review afterward and boom: there you are, reading aloud your inner voice!

1. Write down your situation

You will need a *separate piece of paper*. At the top of this page (leave some spacing for a title you are going to add later on), write down **what is bothering me right now and what do I want to change?** Just leave it there, put your pen down, and read that question to yourself once more. Put both of your feet on the ground, close your eyes, and wait until "something" pops up in your mind related to the question. (This can take seconds, minutes or one hour. although if it takes more than one hour, something went wrong). Just write down whatever comes up. Literally, everything that comes up, it does not have to make sense, write it down. Trust your intuition and trust what you are writing down is what you want to change at this moment. Trust. Really. Trust.

If you have not done this kind of exercises before, it can feel a bit awkward. However, give it a go.

The reason why you are doing it this way is that your mind can immediately respond to this kind of questions. However, I want you to respond to it from your intuition. Otherwise, there is a chance that you are going to transform superficial parts of your life, but in essence, you will not access a more pure state of being. Moreover, that is the thing with your intuition: it will not lie to you.

Keep in mind that all the steps of this course can be done repeatedly. So if you are surprised that your story is missing something, do not be afraid. You can always add something or do it all over again after a while.

Are you done with all the writing? Good!

2. Summarize

Now you have written down your situation, remember that it still needs a title. Make sure it is a one-liner. A conclusion of the story you have just written down as "What do I want to change." Each time you read this title in the upcoming time, you will remember what it stands for. In addition, it will remind you of that thing that you want to change!

Answer this question now in one sentence based upon the title and story you have just created:

Question: What are you doing right now that you are going to change?

Answer:

....

3. Feel the power of change

Now you have written it all down, have it on paper and given it a title, you can start to call in your power and courage to make the change! It is already so brave that you are putting it all into words and you are making clear to yourself what you want to change! To become aware of where you are right now is such a big, important and sometimes, a confronting step. It can look huge, or it can be something small. It does not matter that much, and the process is going to be awesome anyway!

Fold your paper(s) in half and put them aside for later. Done!

As mentioned before the "key" is to direct the unlimited amount of life force that is available towards a different/new direction. By feeding the story that, you have just written down to yourself. So, let us start with that now! I know you have not decided the direction where you want the energy to flow, which has been taken care of in the next chapter! For now, focus yourself on the power that got you here. Your will, your inner guidance, and your intuition. See it as a valuable source of knowledge and as an unlimited source of that awesome energy that you will use to transform! Attached you find an empowerment meditation to listen to at the very end of this chapter.

Empower yourself!

Attached to this chapter, you can find a URL that links to an empowerment meditation created by Bentinho Massaro. It is a short fragment of around 4 to 5 minutes. Every single day, you are going to play this audio for yourself. It will remind you of your greatness, of your power and the power that you hold within you to transform into whatever you want in life, to achieve your dream life!

How you listen to it is not that important, you can either sit down in a chair, sit on the ground, lay down, the most important thing to do is **how** you listen to the audio. Try to pay attention, and minimize the distraction. This means that for some, it can be useful to sit in a quiet space, with your eyes closed. Especially at first, when you are new to this kind of practice, this can be a very good tip: a quiet space, and with your eyes closed.

Now that you have a clear image on what to do in this last step, I will be honest that the title of this part should have been, "Meditate." However, that sounds so scary and boring at times. Although meditation is literally, what I have just described above, sit still for a period putting your attention towards something specific (or towards nothing, which is also a thing). For the process of manifestation, we are going to use the technique of meditation to put your focus on manifesting what you want. We will talk more about it in the chapter "Choose your life."

I love to use the empowerment meditation created by Bentinho Massaro, but feel free to use any kind you prefer.

https://youtu.be/IpvvpovoNTs - Imagineer Your Life (Manifestation Tool)

or https://www.stijnheymans.be/videos

What to do

- ❖ Listen to your intuition and write down "What's bothering me right now and what do I want to change" in my current situation.
- ❖ Write down a title that suits your story.
- ❖ Focus on your strength to transform into awesomeness. Listen to the empowerment audio file.
- ❖ Answer the question: "what are you doing right now that you are going to change?"

Manifestation tools you've used this time

1. Writing
2. Reading
3. Meditation

Know what you want

It is time to transform what you have written down in the previous chapter into something that you want. This does not mean that the situation you are in right now is "not good" or "bad." No, it is just not right for you **at this time** of your life. This is something we will discuss more in detail in one of the next chapters, "Everything is a choice."

In this chapter, the focus is on knowing what you want. It seems like an easy question, yet it is so hard to answer for many people. Moreover, by answering, I mean a proper, detailed answer about what you want in life. Answering: "I don't want my current situation; everything else is fine by me" is not what you are looking for right now!

In the previous chapter, you have written down the things you do not want any more in your life. Therefore, that part is covered. Now it is time to transform all of that into the awesomeness that you want!

> *Focus upon the essence of what you want*
> *to manifest. Not on a specific outcome.*

If everyone knew what he or she - in detail - want in his or her life, everything would be different here on planet earth. When you ask a bunch of people: what do you want? They will answer you with "more money," "more happiness," "more fun," "a happy relationship,", although those things are good starting points, you need to be much more clear to yourself, be specific and dare to dream big – but be aware that you don't limit the power of creation by your own limiting beliefs.

Learning outcome

You will have a clear overview where you want to direct your energy towards, and this allows you to phrase a title that summarizes it all.

What do you want the most?

You know what you don't want, but what is it that you do want? There is an important notion that you have to keep in mind when writing down your desires later on.

Focus yourself upon the essence of what you want to manifest. Not on a specific outcome. Let us say that when I ask you the question: what do you want? The first thing that comes to your mind is a Ferrari. Great! A Ferrari, but dig deeper. A Ferrari is already a very specific physical outcome and excludes other possible awesomeness (such as a Tesla, or a Bugatti).

Why do you want a Ferrari?

Scenario 1
Ahh... Do you want to be rich? Okay, how do you define "being rich"?

Being rich = having abundance, going out for dinner, buying what I need without checking my bank account

Scenario 2
Ahh... Do you want to be seen? Okay, why do you want to be seen while driving around? Do you like to be ignored? Okay, what scares you the most when you are not heard/ ignored?

I could go on writing all kinds of other real-life scenarios all based on the same answer on "what do you want" question. However, as you notice, everyone's essential feeling that is related to the same answer is different, and it is exactly that essence that you need in this chapter. That is where you are going to direct that unlimited life force of yours. The reason that it is important to direct life force to that essence is that you do not want to limit yourself focusing upon one specific thing that *you* just made up as a representation of your desire. That representation is limited by your own limiting beliefs.

Scenario 1

The abundance does not have to come in the form of a million-dollar bank account and Ferrari's all over the place. For some, 1 million dollars is abundance; for others, that is nothing. The same applies to 10k of 1k. 100k or 50k. It is all about your feeling. Regardless of the numbers in your bank account, you can experience way more abundance with just 10k in it than you can with 100k.

Scenario 2

Remember that the answer was: "A Ferrari." Well, apparently, in this scenario, freedom is what the person is looking for. What is freedom exactly? It is an option that you can explore. Although in this particular course, when you combine it with the exercise of chapter one, you can get a grip on what freedom stands for. Again, what freedom exactly looks like is currently still unknown and will stay unknown until the manifestation is paying off.

Being authentic

This part is what I believe is one of the most important things of this entire course: be authentic. *Especially for men,* this is something very important to keep in mind.

You are creating more amazingness in your life by following everything that is provided in this course. Nevertheless, let me be clear for finally about creating awesomeness: it is not about "showing everyone how great your life is according to the social standards." It is about creating **your version of life** for yourself. You are focusing on the most awesome version of what you want to create for yourself. We all have a vision on what "an awesome life" means through the eyes of the world. It has so many different forms that are different for everyone. Keep in mind that you are doing this for yourself. Someone else does not have to find your creation equally great. As long as it is perfect for you, you are doing great! Again, this has to do with perspectives. I like to travel, for instance, so I find that awesome. Maybe traveling is not something you want to do full-time. That **is awesome too**!

Being authentic also means that everything is allowed. There is room for emotions, processes, or lessons to be learned. And if you are just getting started to manifest some completely different from what you have right now: it can be a bumpy road. It does not have to be, but there is a chance since you are stretching your comfort zone.

Authenticity is something relatively unknown in our everyday lives. For both men and women, there are other struggles within authentic awesomeness.

What does it mean to be a "real man?" What does it mean to be a "real woman?" There is so much more to talk about, but for in this book, get familiar with the concept of being authentic awesome, which is the same for both men and women.

Do not stuff away feelings back down inside yourself that come up while manifesting. Explore them, question them and most importantly, be aware of them. When dealing with it, you lift an emotional burden from your shoulders, and you will find some emotional strength and fuel in it!

Authentic awesomeness: Create a version of life that is extraordinary for yourself, regardless of what others think. Whatever comes up during the process of creation is fine. This can be a success, lessons to learn, emotions, or feelings that are stuck at some stage. All is good.

Sharing your version of life with others contains both fun and not so fun feelings. Be authentic and real about it. That is what authentic awesomeness means.

How do I know what I want

Step 1 - Write down what you want

Again, you can spend as much time on as you want in this writing exercise. Like all chapters, it is up to you to decide how much time you are going to need to put this all down into words. I spent around 10-15 minutes on my first draft. You can modify your "what I want" story at every moment in life. Life changes continuously, so what you want changes as well. Fine-tune during the next day's your "what I want" story, and at the end of this course, you will be all set for the upcoming time to manifest what you have written down.

Remember scenario 1 and 2 from above; keep it in mind when you are writing down what you want from life.

If you are having a hard time defining what you want, you can use your story from the previous chapter as a starting point.

Question the things you do not want anymore and write down how you do see it!

Step 2 - Read your own what-I-want-story

Once finished, read it once more to verify whether you have written down the essence of it all instead of an outcome. If you notice you haven't been writing down the essence, dig a bit deeper until you feel that which represents what you want, deep inside.

Step 3 - Visualize

Multiple options are available for you now, and the choice is up to you. Either you can read your story for 5 minutes at least, or you can sit still with your eyes closed.

In both cases, you must **feel** yourself living that version of what you have written down. Of course, this visualization will be based on your best knowledge available to you at this very moment. However, that is okay, although there is a chance that the actual manifestation will come in different forms. Feel it, visualize it. By doing this, you will already get a sense of how it feels like once manifested. If you can imagine it, it means that it is already is a genuine part of your reality.

Step 4 – Empower

Now that you reminded yourself in step 3 which reality you want to switch to, you're going to remind yourself again of your creative power by listening to the empowerment audio file (mentioned in the previous chapter - Empower yourself!).

What to do

- ❖ Write down what you want in life on an essential level
- ❖ Read your own story at least one more time and optimize it – if needed
- ❖ Sit still for at least 5 minutes while reading/ visualize the story you've written down
- ❖ Listen to the empowerment meditation (mentioned in the previous chapter)
- ❖ Answer the question on the template paper "What do you want at this moment in your life."

Manifestation tools you've used this time

1. Writing
2. Reading
3. Visualization
4. Meditation

Unconscious to conscious

In the previous chapters, you made it clear to yourself of what you want to transform into something new, and you have described what it feels like when you will have it. Superb!

In my point of view, one of the trickiest parts of the

whole manifestation process is over now. I am not saying that everything will transform in a snap from now on. Nevertheless, really, it is hard to figure out what you want in life. In addition to take this responsibility and decide how you want your life to look like instead of sending out mixed signals so obvious mediocre/random things. Now you know where to put your focus on. The direction to which the unlimited life force will flow.

In this book, I will share some more about the unconscious to conscious process. Since this is the starting point, from which you are going to start manifesting.

I have already shared it earlier in this text: "decide how you want your life to look like instead of sending out mixed signals to manifest mediocre/random things." I actually mean, now you will consciously create your life instead of leaving it up to your unconsciousness, which makes a huge difference!

This chapter is all about being aware of your unconsciousness. Deal with it and transform it into conscious actions. See it this way: while you are growing up, being educated, and living your life, a whole set of beliefs are installed within yourself. Some of them are good and useful. Others are not serving and can hold you back. The beliefs that you know that were being installed are the easy ones to deal with... Since you **know** that at some level, someone told/educated you on this belief.

Example: you have to work hard to earn lots of money.

Knowing these limiting beliefs makes it relatively easy to anticipate on them since you are aware that this has been taught to you at some point in your life. Living the awesome-lifestyle, invites you to question every belief that you have been taught during your life and ask the question: **is this something I want to hold on to or not?** This is an important question: do I want to hold on to a belief or not?

I am implying that this is an important notion: not all beliefs are bad, of course! Many life lessons that I have learned through my life are valuable to me, and I keep them alive in my reality since I find that they serve me well.

Therefore, that is the "easy" part: locating the unconscious beliefs that you have consciously learned from someone else – society, and teachers …

"Easy" since it is not that simple to recognize that you are acting upon something the way someone taught you years ago when you were a kid.

Next, there is the much more complicated part. Here it comes: locating the unconscious beliefs that you have unconsciously learned from someone else – society, and teachers …

This means that you have not learned it directly from someone or something; you indirectly made assumptions in life. Until now! Often situations like this are related to society or the way your parents raised you. You just saw a certain way of life. You just saw how someone handled a situation etc. All those situations are stored in your sub consciousness, and they made you the person you are right now.

How do you recognize those unconscious beliefs from which you are creating your reality? The answer is by reading life and the way that you react upon it.

Learning outcome

You will be aware that everything that happens is created by yourself, conscious, or unconscious. Knowing that you will be able to learn why things are happening to you and how best to follow them.

Everything happens for a reason

You can find thousands of quotes on the internet that say: Everything happens for a reason. But what does that mean exactly? Well, when you start to read your life, you will start to see the truth of this powerful quote.

Finding unconscious beliefs that were not directly taught to you often show up as life lessons. Life lessons where you can discover and let go of those limiting beliefs that are holding you back at this very moment. If what you've written down as "what I want to manifest" it is something out of your comfort zone or something that is not part of your reality right now is probably a life lesson that will show up.

Awesome does not necessarily mean "fun" when talking about life lessons. It can be confronting or scarify to let go of beliefs that are not serving you. However, I promise, in the end, you will be so fulfilled by stretching and enlarging your mind.

> *You do not always have to feel awesome.*
> *However, you can stay open to*
> *awesomeness all the time.*

Life lessons

It is a fact that life **wants** you to succeed. Regardless of how you define "life." Call it the universe, a specific god, or your actual surroundings such as friends, family; every single aspect of life wants you to live to the fullest and to become the best version of yourself.

When it comes to education, teachers are sometimes pushing their students towards their full capacity. If you continuously score well on a specific course, the chances are that you will get more challenging tasks the next time compared to the other students. Teachers do this because they feel that you are capable of achieving more... Therefore, it is really a generous act from them. They want you to use your full capacity. They *see* you where you maybe cannot see yourself, yet. There is a "but" in this story. Since not all students realize that it is for their own good that the teacher is pushing their limits, the student can feel this "act of greatness" as a burden on their shoulders. Why are they targeting me? However, it would be significant for the student, in some cases, if he could *know* why the teacher is doing this, and that is why I am telling you now: Life **wants** you to succeed. It does. In addition, yes, that means it will push your boundaries. It does so to *help* you.

Now that is settled, you can start observing what is happening to you in your life. Why is it that you will not be hired for a new job? Maybe it is because you have to do something completely different in life. On the other hand, maybe you need to show some more persistence. That is the hard part about studying life: it is up to you to start seeing the signs since every situation means something different for someone else.

There are many tools out in the world that can help you read your own life if it gets too complicated for yourself. However, later on, in "Choose your life," we will dive deeper into this topic.

What to do

- ❖ Write down beliefs that are related to your manifestation.
- ❖ Observe upon everything that happens to you in life: start reading life – keep track of it in a little notebook or on your smartphone for a while.
- ❖ Re-read your "what I want"- story and visualize it.
- ❖ Listen to this empowerment meditation.
- ❖ Write down the question "What are you creating from your unconsciousness" and answer it.

Exercise

Beliefs that are holding you back:

....

....

....

....

....

....

....

....

....

What do you notice when reading your life?

....

....

....

....

....

....

....

....

....

....

....

....

Manifestation tools you've used this time

1. Reading
2. Writing
3. Visualization
4. Meditation

Everything is possible

I will unfold one of the most important magic tricks in life: Everything is possible. I have been explaining in the previous chapters that you can dream big, and that this is a good thing to do. I encourage you to do so, and I question myself: whom wouldn't want to dream big?

You have probably heard about all of those success stories severally now, stories of how someone achieved their success by working hard for it. How they kept on focusing on their life's purpose, got rejected, kept on going, and somehow ended up with having what they want. Awe-inspiring, right? I think it is amazing to read those success stories. They can give you a superpower boost to keep on dreaming big. One thing that often stands out too much is how hard they have "fought" for it. They kept on going, defeat after defeat. I would have loved it if the author/ person who the success story is about, highlighted how much fun he/she had during that process. Okay, it probably was not all fun at that time; but they kept on going, not because someone told them they **must**, but because they wanted to! They felt inside that it is what they wanted. They *felt* it. And I assure you: that is an incredible feeling. They feel that what you want is for real. Like really very real! The real that keeps you going. So yeah, when you put it down in a book, the conclusion is, you kept on going **because he/she wanted to**! Moreover, that is the beauty of it. At some level, it was not that much of a struggle for that particular person. Probably they *needed* setbacks or other so-called life lessons as described in "Life lessons" in the previous chapter. However, in the end, they achieved what they focused on, they enjoyed the process, because of that, they are what they are right now, and they even enjoy it more!

In this story, there are multiple valuable aspects, which I want to highlight. First, enjoy the process because it does matter to the result of the manifestation. Although it is not always that clear that moment, it happens in your life. Secondly, when reading success stories where someone kept on going and going, it feels that it is required for you to work hard and that that is a negative thing. You do not have to work hard. In addition, work does not have to mean that you would not have any fun. Probably you want to put all your energy into something specific because you like to do it. So is it the right thing to call it "you have to work hard to get what you want"? I do not think so since it is a sentence to which already has so many prejudgments. When I rephrase all of this, it looks like this: when you *feel* for yourself that what you want to manifest keeps feeling right *for you*, you'll want to put all your focus upon that specific thing, and you will be ready to deal with everything that will come up while manifesting it. Even the not so fun moments that come as life lessons towards you.

I feel that that is already a big believe that you have to keep in mind when hearing about success stories or about someone else's process in achieving something. Nevertheless, there is more; does it always has to be like that? That many struggles come along and you have to "fight" your way through? NO! That is not the case. I want to be clear on that: it can be one smooth ride without bumps in the road. It does not have to be a bumpy ride. Both scenarios are equally possible. That is the cool part about this. What it is all about, is the path **you** choose. Are you ready to use the mindset that work can be so great? Or do you need a life lesson to convince you? (e.g., putting yourself into such an awful job without a certain level of fun in it?).

The choice is really up to you, in essence,
that is how simple it is... really

Learning outcome

You will dare to dream big, without limitations. Everything is possible. You will have a better point of view on what you desire when you dare to dream big.

Parallel realities

Get yourself ready, because parallel realities are one of the coolest things ever! Parallel realities are a fundamental thing of "daring to dream big." Actually, the famous actor "Jim Carey" has shared a story about his life that can be mapped 1 on 1 with the existence of parallel realities. Jim wrote out a cheque of 10 million dollars to his future self for "acting services," and he gave himself three years. Which he did, with the movie "Dumb and dumber."

You can have a look at the Oprah interview yourself if you find this hard to believe.

https://www.youtube.com/watch?v=nPU5bjzLZX0 - What Oprah Learned from Jim Carrey

or https://www.stijnheymans.be/videos

Hey, here we go: what is a parallel reality? Picture yourself on how a movie is made. A movie exists of multiple frames displayed at a certain speed (frame rate). That is how a movie shows moving images, showing quickly static (not moving) images. The same applies when you draw a character on the first page of a bloc note and draw it repeatedly with a slight difference in the next pages. When you flip the pages quickly, the character will move accordingly.

A movie shows images *sequentially*. First image 1, next image 2, image 3, and so on until the last image. Now cut loose each frame of the movie, so you have separate frames/ images. Swirl them around and imagine just picking up one image. Now you can see that this image is a context of its own. You do not need all the other images to get a clear vision on what the image is about. Right? Therefore, what I am trying to say is that all of the images are standalone by themselves and they do not need to be related with the next or previous image. Moreover, that is a good thing. Because instead of putting all the frames sequentially behind each other, by knowing that the images are not related to each other, you can place the images vertical instead of horizontal.

By doing that, you are getting a clear view of how a parallel instead of what a sequential reality looks like.

It is clear that you can choose *at every moment in* life which image/frame comes next. Since the frames are standalone's and they, do not have to be related to each other. I am saying, "They don't have to" because frequently it looks like they are related. That is just our system of believing that makes them related. Achieving what you want: does it have to take years before you get it? It does if that is what you believe. Now that you know that you can choose out of an unlimited number of upcoming frames, you do not have to wait for years.

> *All situations in life are standalone's by themselves. They do not need to be related to the previous or the next situation*

Yeah, I hear you wonder: but if I want to move to, let us say from Belgium to the south of Spain. Then I cannot just be there in a snap! And I will agree with you on that one: **currently**, no one can achieve that in just a snap. Some of our beliefs are harder to bend than others. However, why would it not be possible? If you are not mastering time traveling yet, moving from Belgium to Spain requires some mandatory frames for you before getting to Spain. Mandatory frames for **your** reality at this time of your being/humankind. Which is, at the time of writing: getting yourself to the airport (bus/train/car), taking a plane to Spain and taking another transportation (bus/train/car) to the final destination. Done.

The speed at which you are putting these required frames into your vertical timeline is up to you. It can take you weeks to close the chapter of your Belgian life and start a new chapter in Spain or you could be there within 24hours. You act upon the speed that feels right for you at that moment in your life. Now that you are aware that means, you are the one that chat speed, and you can start transforming into awesomeness way faster than ever before!

What to do

- ❖ Write down your biggest superhero (can be anyone). Be specific what you admire about that character
- ❖ Re-read your "what I want"-story
- ❖ Listen to the empowerment meditation
- ❖ Answer the question on the template paper "What kind of belief is limiting your creation?"

Exercise

Who is your biggest superhero, and why?

....

....

....

....

....

....

....

....

....

....

....

....

....

....

Manifestation tools you've used this time

1. Reading
2. Writing
3. Visualization
4. Meditation

Up until now, you have already made huge steps and have a more clear vision on 1: what you want for yourself in your life and 2: how you can see results quickly.

It has been quite theoretical until now. In this chapter, I am going to share with you some practices that can help you go through the whole transformation process. Practices that will help you discover parts of yourself that are holding you back while manifesting your awesome life. Other techniques will help you to ease your mind or get a more clear vision on what you want. These are daily practices. The more you do them, the better. However, this does not mean that it has to feel like a "drill." That would not make any sense at all since you are aiming for a lifestyle instead of a "quick fix." Since that quick fix will not fix the initial problem, it is like comparing western medicine with a holistic approach, for instance: Chinese medicine. I have been 100% part of this "quick fix" approach myself. I had physical complaints, went to a doctor who gave me some drugs to suppress it, and I kept going. In many situations, this can help, although it is maybe – in my opinion – not the way to go: it 'can' work. Nevertheless, in a lot of other cases, such as my personal experience the "quick fix" method works instantly, but the problem keeps on repeating itself in the long term. That is not what we are aiming for with this course.

Learning outcome

You will develop your way to maintain believing and to manifest your dreams. A daily routine that suits your lifestyle and personality. You will have a practical guide that empowers you, gives you hope, and inspires you.

Morning ritual

Another powerful tool is having a morning ritual. Having this, it can be life changing. Everything I have discussed in the previous chapters comes in handy during a morning ritual. It is a good way to implement and embody the awesome-lifestyle! For me, it does not matter when you are implementing these tools into your everyday life. For me, morning hours is the most powerful time of the day to do whatever I feel like doing. Morning hours can set a tone for the day. I feel and love that. But if it is not your thing, and you can practice at night, hold on to it through your whole day: that is fine too!

When going through some of the exercises, you will notice that you have already done a lot of them during the past chapters. I have always listed them under the sections "manifestation tools you've used." Combining all of them, and especially focusing on it for some time **makes changes** into your reality. It is the best to manifest what you already feel within yourself into a reality that you experience.

Act upon what you feel inside

There is a book, completely devoted on morning rituals: "Miracle Morning" by Hal Elrod. He came up with the "life S.A.V.E.R.S," which is a great way to remember the tools on how you are going to speed up the manifestation process of your ideal life. In that particular book, it is recommended to spend 10 minutes a day, to each of the life S.A.V.E.R.S topics. Which results in a powerful morning practice of 1 hour a day. Some may not like the idea of one full hour a day on manifesting something new! Yes, *only* 1 hour a day. We are talking about your life. Therefore, if you want to change things into more awesomeness, then you can see the importance of the 1-hour/daily practice. You are committed to living your perfect life all day long. It is good to keep the mindset that it is not that much time to change something into your reality. Of course, your life keeps on going when you are in the process of transformation; that is why it seems like a big job. And for some days, it will feel like a big job to spend time on creating something new.

I am not forcing you into a daily 60 minutes practice. Although I am motivating you with the idea, that it is a very valuable practice for many people. If a daily practice is something you have not done yet (until now) in your life: do not panic. The best way is to start it gradually, and before you even know it: you have a daily practice. Think about it, if you have followed the exercises of the previous chapter, you are already doing it!

1. It's not mandatory

One of the best ways to install a new habit is to realize that it is not mandatory at all. You do not **have** to do it. It is your choice. We will talk more of this in the next chapter, "Everything is a choice," but I want to highlight it here so that you will be familiarized with it. Be gentle with yourself and enjoy your choice. It will start and accelerate the transformation that you want to achieve. Trust the process.

2. Tools

Here is an overview of things that will help you in creating what you want:
- Silence
- Affirmations
- Visualization
- Exercise
- Reading
- Scribing (= Writing)
  - Life S.A.V.E.R.S.

I will dive into each one of them with tangible details. However, without you noticing, you have already put almost all of them into practice. The thing is to keep on diving deep into it. Keep it going if you feel the upcoming "something has to change"-emotion.

It is a good thing to use these tools each day for the rest of your life from now on. However, be aware: you might have a hard time to digest all creations! Although everything is possible, of course. Everything is at its best when it is balanced. In addition, it is also the same case with all the knowledge and the tools you have gathered out of this course. It is okay to take a break from manifesting from time to time, sit back, and relax. After some enjoyment of the manifestation that you have pulled off, you will *feel* it when you will have to start manifesting BIG again. Translating this into the tools and your everyday life: it means that you will be using the tools constantly, but its intensity will change according to your procedure.

Reading

Yoga for the mind is such an important thing to do when you are stretching your reality. As mentioned before, you create your reality on the best knowledge available to you at that moment of your life. If you do the math, you will read 10 pages every day, 365 days in a year: 3650 pages per year. That is at least 10 books.

While reading new and inspiring books, you stretch your knowledge and your beliefs about life. Once you are aware of this, you can start focusing on your version of the newly acquired information and start the manifestation process repeatedly, if that is what you feel.

A book is such an amazing source of information. It is not always possible to attend live events, workshops or meet the speaker in real life. However, all the knowledge that the author of which you want to know more about is bundled into a 300 pages summarization of what he wants to share with you. How amazing is that (and in fact: it is one of the cheapest ways too)! If you are not a reader, that is fine too. There are so many ways to practice mind-yoga, ways like the use of documentaries, YouTube, articles, are perfect too.

Silence

We talked about meditation earlier during this course. It is a powerful tool to ease your mind when you are feeling stressed or unbalanced. And with silence, I refer to the same. Silence, in this context, means silence for your mind. Meditation does not have to be 100% quite; there are many ways to meditate. Regarding the one where you sit still, I love to have a guided meditation. This kind guides you through some steps to bring silence in your mind.

Meditation

You have already been doing some meditation in the previous chapters, the empowerment meditation. However, of course, there are many possibilities. It all depends on what you want to achieve. However, in this course, you are using the power of meditation to manifest something new. Another possibility is to calm your mind and become "mindful." Another one is "transcendental" meditation. Which leads literally to what it says, it lets you transcendent and realize that you are neither your body nor your mind.

What your style, needs, or preference is, is very personal and needs some experimenting. Here are my top-meditation techniques in those three categories (there are way more categories, but I only stated these three for now.).

- ❖ Transcendental: https://youtu.be/wHnl_XugJyE - Isha Kriya (or https://www.stijnheymans.be/videos)
- ❖ Empowerment: https://youtu.be/IpvvpovoNTs - Imagineer Your Life (or https://www.stijnheymans. be/videos)
- ❖ Mindfulness: sit still in silence for 15min. It is nice to have an app for that on your phone, such as "The mindfulness app."
- ❖ Do you need guided mindfulness meditations in Dutch? Check out www.evadaeleman.be

Gratitude

All starts with showing gratitude. That is meditation and lifestyle 1 0 1. Be grateful in life, even if things "happen" to you that you do not like, be grateful. When you start focusing upon gratefulness, you will see great things coming your way. Find that place in your heart where you can feel gratitude. Really feel it. I highly recommend implementing gratitude into your daily meditation.

A specific Hawaiian meditation technique, called "Ho'oponopono" is an awesome guided meditation to practice this.

https://youtu.be/CUHf4dmslro - Jason Stephenson - Gratitude Spoken Meditation | Ho'oponopono Ancient Hawaiian Prayer

or https://www.stijnheymans.be/videos

Timing

Since every day is different, and sometimes you have more time than other days for meditation, it is easy to pick a meditation duration that suits you.

- ❖ Long (20-30min): Gratitude (15min), silence (5min), empowerment (5min)
- ❖ Medium (10min): Silence (5min), empowerment (5min)
- ❖ Short (5min): Empowerment (5min)

Writing

Write down the parallel reality that you have in mind. While writing, feel it and write it down as you are already writing from the experience of being it. It is a letter that describes you in a situation where you want to be. The fact that you can see it/feel it means that you already going to the right direction. It is already a part of you, but your surroundings have not adapted to it accordingly.

1. Write down the most accurate description of what you want to manifest — your awesome **parallel life**.
2. You will notice that when you are creating the best version of yourself, new things will come up down the road. Write down positive affirmation upon these smaller, yet important steps of the lifestyle that you are creating. These **transportation steps** are an important part!

Imagine the path of creation that I have described above is the same as you traveling to some other country:

You are already aware of why you want to go to that other space. *It is already part of your imagination; thus, it is part of your reality.* That place where you want to go is just waiting for you in another parallel reality. Thus, you could go instantly to that place, without taking a train, bus or plane.

The description of this could look like this:
I live in a place on earth where I can enjoy being under the sun, and where it gets cold during the night for a good rest...

When you are trying to manifest your being in the other country, you'll discover that new things will come up such as in this case: you will not be able to time travel (yet): instant switching between you being in one place on earth and then you being somewhere else on earth in the next second. Thus, you write down a positive affirmation upon it, which gets you there by using the best possible option that you know of *right now*.

I travel in style. I enjoy the time that it takes me to get from place A to place B. While I travel in luxury, it nourishes my being, and I arrive at my destination all charged up.

Exercise- Body movement

Instead of yoga for the mind, by body movement, I refer to yoga for the body. Does it have to be yoga? Nope, as long as you are doing some body movement. That could mean swimming, running, and cycling ... Although I have to say that some yoga has many benefits to your being. You are focusing upon breath and movement while doing yoga. I am not saying you cannot consciously cycle or run, and it is just a matter of being focused and yoga is already a mindful/conscious lifestyle.

Food

Another important factor that I did not mention in an everyday book about morning rituals is food.it is such a vital factor. I have already mentioned food earlier. Just make it part of your daily practice. If you are not able – for whatever reason to apply any of the tools I am providing you with, make an effort to do the food part anyways... Really! It is what gives you power through the whole day, you know!

Awesome food

Yes, if you are asking me that is a thing! It is easy to define what awesome food is:

- ❖ Unprocessed foods
- ❖ No added sugar
- ❖ No toxics, such as alcohol
- ❖ Plant-based

Done!

Unfortunately, the sad news is that it can be a struggle to find such foods. Somehow we ended up in a world where **real food** is hard to find and is often more expensive than crappy food that you can find everywhere. The biggest difference between real and crappy food is, of course, the amount of energy you get from it! As I told you before, you can use all the amount of nutrition that real food provides when you are forming your awesomeness!

Did you know that sugar is seven times more addictive than cocaine? In addition, it drains your energy level instead of boosting it. That is crazy!

Alcohol... How to start on that one. The same as with sugar, everyone knows that it is not *the best* for themselves. You can even have a hangover **the next day**. However, nobody seems to care. Your body wants to get all of the toxins out. Therefore, I do not have to state that you are harming yourself by drinking alcohol, even in small amounts. As with all the rest, we have beliefs and a society that is forming our reality. If you would be very honest with yourself and you would feel the actual impact on your being. Then it would be as simple as this: you would not drink alcohol anymore. Nevertheless, here are some beliefs that are true for many people:

- When you go out, you "have" to drink, why would you go out otherwise?
- You cannot have fun without alcohol.
- It's so cozy to have a glass of wine/beer on a sunny afternoon
- It's delicious combined with meat
- Beer is cool
- Being wasted is cool

None of the things I have listed above is something I want to take for granted into my reality. I had plenty of sugar and alcohol. And when I honestly look back: alcohol and sugar paralyzed my being. It made me feel ok whenever I felt crappy. It let me tuck away inner feelings that I prefer not to feel because I was too scared (and not powerful enough) to face them or deal with them. In addition, it made me look cool and let me do things I was too scared to do so at that moment. At some level, it made all of the fears that were holding me back into being my true self disappear. Which is an awesome and empowering feeling? However, in the end, my being suffered from it. The next day you wake up, and you feel that you are not 100% who you want to be, you feel stuck. Since the only way, you know how to access that (fun) part of you, is to put toxins into your body of which you have to recover for days.

Level of importance

Here is the level of importance which you have to consider when you are about to develop a practice that suits you. Whereas the most powerful ritual is one that includes every step each day, you do not need to implement it all at once. However, when dealing with "creating awesomeness," some of them are more powerful than others. However, eventually, all of them are worth implementing in your everyday life.

(1: most impact)

1. Food
2. Meditation
3. Writing
4. Exercise
5. Visualizations
6. Reading
7. Affirmations

What to do

- ❖ Define your own (morning) practice. Let them contain at least three steps from the six life S.A.V.E.R.S.
- ❖ Practice your ritual each day
- ❖ Eat healthy starting from today
- ❖ Answer the question on the template paper "What actions are you taking?". Next to each action, put a deadline (date) so you can verify if you've achieved it by then. (tip: put it in your calendar)

Manifestation tools you've used this time

1. Food
2. Reading
3. Writing
4. ...

Everything is a choice

Everything is a choice. We tend to forget this important aspect of life and by doing that, we blame others (or life) for the bad things happening to us. It gives us a feeling that we are not in control of our life. It makes us feel powerless, whereas the complete opposite is true.

Let me remind you that everything is a choice of your own and that you are in control of your life. By realizing this fact, I will share the best technique that I use when I want to introduce new habits into my life. Let us say: how I am changing my reality (habits) by making other choices.

Learning outcome

You will learn how you can implement a new habit into your life and keep it alive. You will experience how this can be fun when maintaining it.

You MUST do... nothing!

As mentioned earlier, you are the creator of life. You are in control of your own choices. Thus, of your own life. However, why doesn't it feel like that (anymore)? A lot has to do with self-responsibility. Since it, looks like choices are a sequential thing. You choose one thing, which leads to making a more limited choice in the future. However, as mentioned in one of the previous chapters ("Parallel realities") this makes no sense. After you have made a choice, you have a new choice. And after that choice, you have a completely new choice to make. This means that in essence, making a choice has no impact at all upon the choices that you have to make later. What changes when you make a choice is a possible impact on everything that surrounds you. So yes, making a choice changes the impact of the next choice you have to make. Let us say that you commit (= a choice) to a certain job that you love, and it is a well payed job (whatever that means), so you will have a monthly income. When looking for a place to rent, your previous choice of having a monthly income influences this new choice, and the amount of rent you can afford every month. In this very simple example, you already have two choices in life that are related to each other.

Going even a bit deeper in this hypothetical (but o so realistic) example; At a certain point in life, it becomes possible that you're fed up with your daily job The job that gives you the monthly income and which lets you pay the rent. Again, in essence, it is 100% up to you on what you are going to choose when dealing with this situation. However, since you are dealing with **related choices**, it can feel like a hard call to make, and people tend to say; "I don't have a choice. I MUST ..." But that is nonsense. You do have a choice, but you will have to take responsibility for it. In this particular situation, a possible choice to make can be to keep the job. This will implicitly state that you can keep up the (high?) lifestyle that is related to it. And if that is what you want (the lifestyle) that is fine! Maybe you would think that I would disagree with that kind of choices in life. But I really do not. The notion that I do have to make is that at every moment, you have to **realize that it is your conscious choice!** Doing this, you will be able to enjoy your life even more. You will not be able to complain that you are not doing what you like to do since you are making a conscious choice that you feel that keeping your lifestyle is worth more - for you - than loving what you are doing in your everyday job. That is perfect: you will love your life from the moment you are making the choices consciously.

Apply this technique of being aware that you are choosing everything in your own life (even the thing you may be disliked, but you are choosing for a certain reason). It will step up your game, and you will love life even more!

One of the things that made a huge impact on my life is banning the word "must" out of my vocabulary since "I must" do nothing at all. Must I get some veggies at the supermarket? Nope, I want to get them – otherwise, I do not have food for dinner. I must leave. Nope, I want to leave, because I will have to pick up friends from the airport. They do not force you to do it.

1. Commitment

I feel that I need to add a section about commitment when talking about "everything is a choice." When I am sharing this with you, you could think, but isn't it egoistic by not picking up your friends from the airport when you committed? The answer is, yes and no. I share a way of life where you will experience more fun in all you do. If it feels for you that you will have to cancel the airport pick up because there is something that will harm your being, then you have a solid reason not to pick them up. However, you are also taking responsibility for it. If done with integrity, they will understand that you need to take care of yourself first. You will take responsibility for your actions. There is a huge difference in letting them know two days or 2 hours before they arrive at the airport. And in either situation, you are taking your responsibility. Whereas that can mean that – in the case of 2 hours upfront notice – means handling with your friends being angry with you.

How to implement a new habit

The trick in implementing new patterns to empower your being is that you are choosing to implement them, and nobody is forcing you. Not even yourself. When trying to apply valuable practices as we discussed in the previous chapter of a Morning ritual, practices such as meditation, healthy food, this is a valuable lesson. Combine the realization that everything is a choice, with listening to your body is a match made in heaven. First, a period of 30 days is needed to "kick-off" from the old, or implement the new. And during these 30 days, you are allowing your body and mind to settle with the new pattern of your life. You are giving it signals that you are changing. Depending on what you will want to implement, you will need some willpower to get it through to the end of the 30 days.

See it like this: your being is testing you to ascertain if this new habit is **really,** what you want. (It does not like change; remember). The first 30 days, you will have counted upon your willpower to get through this. However, after these 30 days, you will be changed, and you will be able to read very honestly, what it is that is serving you or not.

Let us say you want to start eating healthy food, which is an everyday routine. To be more specific, you want to go sugar-free (I recommend it). Therefore, day 1, you stop eating sugar (not only stop eating cookies, but also no pre-made meals that contain refined sugar). And as I said earlier, sugar is quite addictive, so the first 30 days, you will find yourself craving for it. When you are going out to get yourself a nice cup of tea, the cookie that comes along with it will try to get all of your attention. My trick was to ask politely to take the cookie immediately back with them when they would bring my order. However, after the 30 days, something happens.

The cookie comes along, but it has no voice anymore. It stopped shouting out to me. That is the turning point. You have reclaimed back the power of choice; you will always have a choice. From now on, when a cookie comes, you are cool with that. Nevertheless, I will be honest, at some point, there is going to be a certain moment when you will feel that you are just torturing yourself by not eating the sugary things. You have been clean on sugar for two months, and then you are all of a sudden in such a cozy restaurant where you had the best dessert *ever* years ago. Again, you have a choice: to eat it, or not to eat it. You can choose not to eat it, but maybe you would regret it afterward... When applying a new habit like this in your life, it often feels like a struggle, a fight. So, in this same scenario, remind yourself that you have a choice. So try it again, eat it and enjoy it while eating it!

Once done, get into your feeling what it is bringing you. Is it as yummy as you had imagined? Did you have more energy afterward? Or do you feel more nervous? Be honest with yourself. Next time, when you have the same choice in eating it or not, you can keep in mind the feeling that came up to the last time you ate the cookie. And out of my own experience, it often lets me realize that I have a choice and that the choice of eating it, ends up in having a less awesome feeling. So then, I choose not eating it.

This process of choice, "to eat" or "not to eat" keeps on repeating. When I became a vegetarian, I did not eat meat for one week. After that week, I ended up in a situation (probably a restaurant) where I wanted to have meat. So I ordered it). However, I genuinely felt like: this is not *the* best thing for my body. Therefore, again one week later, I felt the same craving, but my being reminded me of the conclusion of the week before. Therefore, I chose the vegetarian option. Once again, a week later, I felt the craving again: but this time, I started doubting my lesson of 2 weeks ago. Therefore, I gave it another go. But once more, my body told me: no. Okay, okay, lessons learned. Again, one week later, a craving; this time I could remember the lesson. Another week later – craving – I could remember the lesson. Another week later – craving – I could remember the lesson. Another week later – craving – I could remember the lesson. Another week later – craving – I started doubting my lesson of 4 weeks ago. Therefore, I gave it another go. However, did you notice that the period I had no meat at all became longer and longer? It rapidly increased! Eventually, you fluently install a new pattern into your life without even struggling, because at each phase, you are reminding yourself that you are the one making the choice. No one is forcing you; you want this for yourself. For your being. You are all in!

Game on!

What to do

- ❖ Pay attention to your language, don't use the word "must" anymore
- ❖ Apply your routine from the previous chapter into your daily life.

Law of attraction

You are what you give – Karma is awesome

Once I heard a kid saying aloud: "Karma is a b*tch." Her saying that intrigued me, so I questioned what she meant with it. So she explained: "when doing bad things, something bad will happen to you as well. So if you're bullying someone, there's a big chance that you'll get some of that in return."

Superb, she knows what karma is all about. Although there was an important notion, she missed. The phrase "karma is a bitch" is widely used. I explained that she was completely right with her explanation, but I invited her to turn it around: Karma is awesome. When you are doing something awesome for someone else, something awesome will happen to you as well. Isn't that awesome?

That is literally, what the law of attraction is all about. You are what you give. Whatever you surround yourself with is what you will attract. If you are transforming into your manifestation, then start surrounding yourself with that kind of energy. Do you want to become a pilot, hang out at the airport? Follow a workshop, "start to paint." Meet people who are living as digital nomads, Surround yourself with those things that you want or want to become.

Learning outcome

You will learn that sharing is caring. How you can contribute to a collective while you are taking care of yourself at the same time.

Enjoy now, and focus on the future

If you are already at some level familiar with teachings related to empowering, self-help books or self-development you've probably heard of "be present," "the power of now", ... If you haven't heard of it, well there's a lot (really a lot) of interesting lecture about it. However, it all comes down to this: enjoy every moment to the fullest. Be present in every moment, and you will feel more joy in everything you do. Do not worry about the past or the future. It is worth learning more about the power of now because the society has forgotten how important it is. Not everyone is present anymore, for instance, in a face-to-face conversation. While talking to each other, we are wondering or worrying about other stuff, or maybe we are texting at that very moment with some else. So yeah, being present is important!

How about that focus upon the future? Isn't that "not being present"?

Past present vs. Future present

Here is the deal: being present is important since it will let you enjoy each moment to the fullest. Even if you are still in the process of manifesting something new! However, there are different ways to be present that can make a huge difference when you are designing your own life.

1. Past present

If you aren't aware of how to manifest more of what you want in your life, the approach of "past-present" can be the one that you are holding on to this very moment.

As discussed through this course, you are going to manifest something new by focusing on it and attracting it into your life. The law of attraction gives you what you focus yourself on. Therefore, when you are just present without knowing which direction you are heading towards, you are recreating your past repeatedly. Does that make sense?

You do not know the direction where you are heading to, and you just trust that whatever you need in life (which you are not sure of what that is) will come to you. The law of attraction will thus recreate what you already know/where you are at this time since that is where you are focusing yourself on – the present. Doing this, you will be able to manifest new things, but at a very slow speed, since you are recreating 90% of the past and 10% new things.

2. Future present

Unlike the past present, by living in the future present, you know in essence what you to achieve. You know the direction you want to go. You are enjoying the moment, and you know that each moment is supporting the direction that you are going. It does not mean that you *get* everything that is happening at you at every moment. Connecting the dots (= knowing why something happened at a certain point in life), is something you will probably only be able to see after it all happened. By knowing which direction you are pointing the limitless life force towards, you are mostly creating something new in your life. You are creating the life, which you envisioned.

Can you tell the big difference by living in the past or future present? Past present: you are mostly recreating the past. Future present: you are mostly creating new content since you know the direction you are forwarding your energy.

Books

To give you an example of how you can surround yourself with the reality that you are focusing on, I will give you the example of a book.

A book is something that contains lots of wisdom about a particular topic. In a book, you will find all the knowledge the instructor wants to share with you written out for you.

However, a book is just an example. There are, of course, many ways to surround yourself with the reality that you want to manifest; workshops, meetings, skype calls, and friends can also be used. However, considering buying a book, it is like sending out a signal: I am ready for it. You buy the book and is sending out that whatever the book is about is something that you want to attract in your life. You want to learn more about it, and maybe you want to get inspired by it, or whatever. For some, it may not even be important to read the book. Just by buying it, they are already sending out the vibes that they need to attract into their lives.

It looks like such an easy manifestation rule that we are handling in this chapter: surround yourself with what you want to attract. And in fact, it is just that simple. Somehow, it looks too simple that we tend not to believe the simplicity. Experience it that is how simple it is to attract more of it in your life.

Social media

One of the exercises in this course is to go through all of your social media accounts and start following/unfollowing people, pages, or companies. It is a fun metaphor for life, social media, and here is why.

Your Facebook, Instagram, or whatever social media feed represents the choices you have made in the past. You became friends with someone; you have started following some businesses that you found interesting and so on. You know the drill. Therefore, we could state that your feed represents you at some level.

Then there is a time where you have the feeling that your feed is not that awesome anymore. It does not resonate 100% with you anymore. You have changed a lot over the last period, internally, but your feed is still showing you "the old information." So yeah, you know what to do right? If something that does not resonate anymore comes up, you click "unfollow." That is it. But of course, your interests have changed, so for each unfollow that you do, you go to the "search" bar and start looking for the best of what you're passionate about right now. And you start following that one.

You will see the difference the next day. What you have unfollowed will not show up anymore, and instead, you will see a new interesting post about your new passion, which leads you to like another page that is related to it. Of course, there will still be popping up some irrelevant content, so apply the same technique, repeatedly. And oh boy, you'll be surprised how fast your whole feed will change!

That is the law of attraction. Surround yourself with what you want, and more of that will come towards you. The "surrounding yourself with" can mean everything, as mentioned before, books, people, social media, magazines, movies, workshops, YouTube videos...

What to do

- ❖ Do at least one thing every day that makes the world a better place. Example: pick up a piece of trash and throw it in the bin.
- ❖ Live in the future present
- ❖ Go through your social media accounts and start to follow/unfollow people or groups
- ❖ Keep on practicing your (morning) routine into your daily life.

Manifestation tools you've used this time

1. Reading
2. Depends on your practice

Live your awesome life

Remember that this book is never complete or finished. You can re-use all the steps to keep on manifesting. I highly recommend doing that!

There is a beautiful way of life: the 20/80 rule. That is good to keep in mind when manifesting. Always dream big. And know the direction that you are heading. But to see actual (quick) changes in your life, apply the 20/80 lifestyles: if something new scares you for less or equal than 20%, start manifesting it/do it. If it is greater than 20%, chop it down into smaller steps.

Doing this will give you more visible results, which can come in handy for your self-confidence and motivation.

Learning outcome

You will have all the tools, tips, and tricks to transform your life into anything you want. Create your version of the life you want.